Cardinals

Cardinals

Patrick Merrick

THE CHILD'S WORLD®, INC.

Library of Congress Cataloging-in-Publication Data
Merrick, Patrick.
Cardinals / by Patrick Merrick.
p.   cm.
Includes index.
Summary: Describes the physical characteristics,
behavior, habitat, and life cycle of cardinals.
ISBN 1-56766-592-6 (lib. bdg. : alk paper)
1. Cardinals (Birds)—Juvenile literature.
[1. Cardinals (Birds).]   I. Title.
QL696.P2438M47   1999
598.8'83—dc21   98-38134
CIP
AC

Photo Credits

© 1997 Adam Jones/Dembinsky Photo Assoc. Inc.: 30
© Alvin E. Staffan, The National Audubon Society Collection/Photo Researchers: 23
ANIMALS ANIMALS © Breck P. Kent: 2
ANIMALS ANIMALS © Patti Murray: 6
© C. Heidecker/VIREO: 29
© Cliff Beittel: 15
© Dan Sudia, The National Audubon Society Collection/Photo Researchers: cover
© 1993 Gijsbert van Frankenhuyzen/Dembinsky Photo Assoc. Inc.: 19
© 1994 Jim Roetzel/Dembinsky Photo Assoc. Inc.: 20
© Maslowski Photo, The National Audubon Society Collection/Photo Researchers: 24
© 1994 Skip Moody/Dembinsky Photo Assoc. Inc.: 9, 13, 16
© 1995 Stan Osolinski/Dembinsky Photo Assoc. Inc.: 10
© 1996 Stan Osolinski/Dembinsky Photo Assoc. Inc.: 26

On the cover...

Front cover: It is easy to see how beautiful this male cardinal is from up close.
Page 2: This female is resting on a forest branch.

Table of Contents

If you sit quietly in your backyard as the sun begins to set, you might find many different animals. You might hear frogs and crickets, or maybe see a squirrel running up a tree. You might see different kinds of birds, too. As you watch the birds, look for one that is bright red. If you see one, listen for its wonderful song: "CHIRR–CHIRR–PRIT–PRIT–PRIT–PRIT!" What type of bird is this? It's a cardinal.

⇐ This cardinal is chirping in a tree in New Jersey.

What Do Cardinals Look Like?

Cardinals are songbirds. Robins, orioles, wrens, and sparrows are songbirds, too. Besides being able to sing wonderful songs, all of these birds also have four toes on their feet—three in front and one behind. When these birds **perch**, or sit on a branch, they wrap their toes around it to keep from falling off.

This female cardinal is perched on an icy branch. ⇒

Even if a tree is full of birds, cardinals are often easy to spot. That's because the males are bright red. The females are harder to find, though. That's because they are a dull pink color.

Another way cardinals are different from many other songbirds is that they have small feathers on their head that stand straight up. This is the cardinal's **crest.**

Where Do Cardinals Live?

At one time, cardinals only lived in the southeastern United States and Mexico. Today, cardinals can be found almost everywhere in the United States. Some cardinals have even been found as far north as Canada.

Cardinals like to live in small, thick bushes and in evergreen trees. You can find them near water or in the middle of a field. Cardinals also make their homes in city trees.

This cardinal is enjoying the sunshine on a cold winter's day. ⇒

When the weather turns colder, many birds **migrate,** or travel, south. The cardinal, however, does not. As long as this happy little bird has enough food, it stays in the same area, or **territory,** all year long.

Cardinals are very protective of their territories. They try to scare away other birds and animals by flying at them. If that doesn't work, the cardinal goes to a nearby tree and squawks at the unwelcome visitor.

These male cardinals are fighting over a territory in Texas. ⇒

Because of its beautiful red feathers and its pretty song, the cardinal is one of the most popular birds. In fact, the cardinal is the official bird of seven states! Many people enjoy having cardinals in their yards. They set up bird feeders so they can watch cardinals right from their windows. They also put out birdbaths so the cardinals have plenty of water for drinking and bathing.

⇐ This male cardinal is eating seeds at a backyard feeder.

What Do Cardinals Eat?

Cardinals usually eat seeds and fruit. If they are hungry enough, they will also eat nuts, bread, insects, or corn. They will even eat leftover crumbs from your lunch! A cardinal's favorite food is black sunflower seeds. They have been known to go through whole bird feeders just to eat all the sunflower seeds.

A cardinal's beak is well suited for eating seeds. It is short and very strong. The cardinal uses its thick beak much like you would use a nutcracker. It simply picks up seeds and breaks them open by biting down hard.

This female cardinal is cracking a seed in her beak. ⇒

How Are Baby Cardinals Born?

When spring arrives, cardinals begin to look for a mate. To find each other, male and female cardinals sing to each other. The female softly starts a song, and the male loudly copies her. Cardinals love to sing, and they continue singing to each other all day.

After they have mated, the female builds a nest in a safe place. The nest is made of loose twigs and grass. When she is ready, she lays three or four eggs. Two weeks later, the eggs hatch.

⇐ These cardinal eggs are ready to hatch.

What Are Baby Cardinals Like?

Cardinal babies, or **chicks,** look just like their mother. They are a dull pink color that blends in with the nest and other surroundings. Coloring that helps an animal blend in with its surroundings is called **camouflage.** By blending in, the mother and chicks are less likely to be found by an enemy.

This female has just brought some food to her hungry chicks. ⇒

Cardinal chicks leave the nest before they are very good fliers. Sometimes a chick ends up on the ground or far away from its nest. When this happens, it chirps loudly to let its parents know where it is. If you see a small cardinal on the ground, don't pick it up. Its parents will be back soon to help it and give it food.

Cardinal eggs and chicks face many dangers. Female cardinals must protect their eggs from animals such as raccoons and snakes that may try to eat them. When they are still in the nest, young chicks can die if an enemy finds them. Chicks can also die if bad weather comes while they are still small and weak.

⇐ This chick is chirping to tell its parents where it is.

Are Cardinals in Danger?

With all of these problems, some people worry that cardinals may die out someday. However, this is not likely. When their first babies are grown, cardinals mate again. That means that cardinals can have a lot of babies every year. Since there are so many birds having so many babies, there should always be cardinals for people to see.

This male cardinal is feeding his second set of babies. ⇒

Will Cardinals Live in Your Yard?

If you want to see some beautiful cardinals in your yard, there are a few things you should do. First, make sure there are places for the birds to make nests. Small bushes and thick evergreen trees make good homes for cardinals. Then set up a bird feeder. Remember, cardinals love sunflower seeds! Since cardinals don't migrate, you should keep food in the feeder all year long. Then, if you are lucky, you will be able to see whole families of cardinals, even on cold winter days.

⇐ This cardinal has found lots of seeds to eat at someone's feeder.

Glossary

camouflage (KAM–oo–flazh)
Camouflage is colors or patterns that help an animal hide. Cardinals use camouflage to blend in with their surroundings.

chicks (CHIKS)
A chick is a young bird. Cardinal chicks are a dull pink color.

crest (KREST)
A crest is a group of feathers that grow on top of a bird's head. Cardinals have a beautiful crest.

migrate (MY–grate)
When animals migrate, they move from one place to another. Cardinals do not migrate.

perch (PERCH)
When birds perch, they sit on a branch. Cardinals perch to eat and rest.

territory (TARE–ih–tor–ee)
A territory is an area of land that an animal claims as its own. Cardinals often stay in one territory all year long.

Index